TRAVEL GUIDE TO RAMSGATE 2025

Uncover the Magic of England's Coastal Treasure

GEORGE KELLER

TABLE OF CONTENTS

MUST-SEE ATTRACTIONS

- ❖ Ramsgate Royal Harbour
- ❖ Saint Augustine's Abbey and Shrine
- ❖ Ramsgate Maritime Museum
- ❖ The Turner Contemporary

NATURE AND OUTDOORS

- ❖ Pegwell Bay Nature Reserve
- ❖ Parks, Gardens, and Open Spaces
- ❖ Bird watching and Wildlife Spotting

FOOD AND DRINK

- ❖ Traditional Kentish Cuisine
- ❖ Best Seafront Cafés and Pubs
- ❖ Top-Rated Restaurants for Every Budget

SHOPPING IN RAMSGATE

- ❖ Artisan Shops and Boutiques
- ❖ Local Markets and Souvenirs
- ❖ Tips for Unique Finds

LOCAL INSIGHTS AND TIPS

- ❖ Common Phrases and Local Etiquette
- ❖ Avoiding Tourist Traps
- ❖ Insider Recommendations
- ❖ Emergency Contacts and Useful Numbers

CONCLUSION

- ❖ Wrapping Up Your Ramsgate Adventure
- ❖ Share Your Experience!

INTRODUCTION

Welcome to the Coastal Treasure

Ah, Ramsgate! A name that feels like a whisper from the sea. Perched on the southeastern edge of England, this picturesque coastal town provides the ideal blend of history, wildlife, and plain old-fashioned beach fun. Ramsgate, known for its royal harbor (yep, it's posh), golden dunes, and unique blend of old-world elegance and modern vibrancy, is a treasure chest waiting to be opened.

Ponder this: you're standing on a port pier, the salty breeze twisting your hair, birds squawking in greeting as the sun glints off the waters. Ramsgate is more than a destination; it's an experience, a little slice of heaven with a narrative to tell on every street corner.

Ramsgate has something for everyone,

whether you're a history buff, a foodie, a nature lover, or simply want to get away from the hustle and bustle of everyday life. In 2025, it shines brighter than ever before, with new attractions, repaired landmarks, and a vitality that is both fresh and ageless.

Why Visit Ramsgate in 2025?

Why not visit Ramsgate in 2025? This is the year to do it. Ramsgate, with its recently renovated waterfront and packed event schedule, is like that friend who just had a makeover—looking fantastic and ready to show off.

A Harbor Fit For Royalty

Ramsgate's Royal Harbour is the only one in England to have earned royal recognition. (You'll want to mention it at dinner parties later.) It's a lovely sanctuary for yachts and fishing boats, surrounded by small cafés and bars where you can enjoy a coffee or a pint while taking in the scenery.

Sun, Sand, and Sea

Ramsgate has some of the cleanest and most picturesque beaches in the UK. Whether you're building sandcastles with the kids, looking for seashells, or simply relaxing with a good book, the golden sands are screaming your name.

Historical Wonders

History permeates every cobblestone in Ramsgate. From the underground tunnels that previously sheltered hundreds to the stately St. Augustine's Abbey, each turn takes you back in time.

Foodies rejoice!

Ramsgate is quickly becoming a mecca for foodies. Your taste senses will be dancing with delight as you enjoy freshly caught seafood served in dockside restaurants and handcrafted delicacies at local markets.

Events galore

In 2025, Ramsgate will host a number of festivals, including the highly anticipated Ramsgate Festival of Sound. It's a weeklong celebration of music, art, and community spirit. Pro tip: Bring comfy shoes because you'll be dancing.

How To Use This Guide

Let us be honest: travel guides can be overwhelming at times. But don't worry, this one is as simple as walking along Ramsgate's promenade. Consider it your pocket-sized best buddy, loaded with insider information, hilarious commentary, and everything you need to make your vacation memorable.

Here's how to make the best of it:

Plan, but remain flexible

Each element of this tutorial is intended to help you navigate Ramsgate like a professional. Everything from the best times to visit to must-see sights is right here. However, do not feel obligated to adhere to a strict itinerary. Ramsgate has a habit of surprising its guests, so allow for some spontaneity.

Pick Your Adventure

Are you here for the beach, the history, or the food? Perhaps you just want to unwind and soak in the atmosphere. Turn to the portions that speak to your soul. It includes a chapter for locating hidden coves and drinking local beer.

Keep it lighthearted

This guide is intended to be both entertaining and instructive. Expect some humor, personal experiences, and possibly a dad joke or two (sorry, not sorry). For example, have you heard about the seagull who attempted to take my fish and chips? I am still not over it.

Share your experience

Whether you're taking photos in the port or laughing at my corny jokes, I hope this guide contributes to the enjoyment of your Ramsgate vacation. Don't forget to share your favorite sites with friends or online. Ramsgate deserves all of the love.

So there you have it—thc warmest welcome to Ramsgate! By the time you leave, you'll have a wealth of memories and a renewed respect for England's seaside treasures. Let's dive in and discover the enchantment of Ramsgate one wonderful moment at a time.

GETTING TO RAMSGATE

So you've decided to visit Ramsgate. Excellent choice! Now comes the enjoyable part: finding out how to get there. Don't worry, I've got you covered with all you need to know, from picturesque routes to the most effective travel methods. Let's break it down step by step so you can arrive in Ramsgate like a pro.

By Road, Rail, and Air

By Road

If you prefer doing road trips (or simply screaming your favorite tunes with the windows down), traveling to Ramsgate is an excellent choice. The town is well connected to the major road network. The drive from London takes roughly two hours, depending on traffic and how many snack stops you make. The M2 and A299 will be your closest companions on this adventure.

Here's a tip: keep your camera ready for when you reach the seaside stretch. The sights are postcard-worthy, and let's be honest—who doesn't enjoy a good "I am almost there!"Car selfie with the sea in the background?"

By Rail

Ah, trains! The ideal combination of comfort and speed. Ramsgate is well served by Southeastern Railway, which operates regular services from London. If you take the high-speed train from London St. Pancras, you'll be enjoying tea by the harbor in just 1 hour and 15 minutes.

Trains also run from London Victoria and Charing Cross, albeit they take slightly longer. But hey, more time to unwind and admire the rolling countryside sights. Don't forget to take a window seat; you'll travel through some wonderful small villages along the way. Bonus: Ramsgate's rail station is a short taxi or bus trip from the town center.

By Air

Okay, Ramsgate doesn't have its airport (yet!), but don't worry—London's airports have you covered. Gatwick and Heathrow are the nearest major airports. From there, you can take a train or rent a car to complete your journey.

Southend Airport and London City Airport offer a more local experience. They are smaller, quieter, and closer. Ideal if you want to avoid large crowds and long security waits.

Local Transportation Options

Once you've arrived, Ramsgate is surprisingly simple to navigate. It is tiny, walkable, and has plenty of local transportation alternatives to get you where you need to go. Here's a quick rundown:

On Foot

Let's start with the most basic option: your own two feet. Ramsgate's town center and coastline are quite walkable. Strolling down the seafront with the sea breeze in your hair is a must. Plus, you'll burn off all the fish and chips you'll be eating—win-win!

Buses

Thanet's bus network is both efficient and inexpensive. The Loop service connects Ramsgate to nearby Broadstairs and Margate, allowing you to easily explore the entire area. Buses run often, and the drivers are usually nice (though I wouldn't ask them to recommend a pub because opinions differ strongly around here).

Taxis and Ride-sharing

Need to get somewhere quickly? Taxis are widely available in Ramsgate. Local firms, like Central Cars, are dependable and fairly priced. If you're more of an app person, see if ride-sharing services like Uber or Bolt are available during your vacation.

Cycling

If you want to get some exercise, renting a bike is an excellent way to explore Ramsgate and the surrounding area. The Viking Coastal Trail is a popular route that provides breathtaking vistas and the opportunity to explore the best of Kent's coastline. Don't forget to bring sunscreen—it's breezy, but the sun can be sneaky!

Accessibility Tips

Ramsgate is a community that welcomes everyone and is making remarkable steps in accessibility. Whether you have unique mobility needs or simply prefer to plan, here are some useful tips:

Step-free Train Stations

Ramsgate's rail station is wheelchair accessible, providing step-free access to platforms and help on request. It is usually a good idea to tell Southeastern Railway ahead of time if you may want additional assistance.

Accessible Attractions

Many of Ramsgate's most popular sights, like the Royal Harbour, are developed with accessibility in mind. The promenade is flat and easy to access, which makes it ideal for wheelchairs and strollers.

Getting Around Town

Local buses have ramps and dedicated areas for wheelchair users. Taxis can also accept mobility assistance, but you should phone ahead to guarantee availability.

Beach Access

While some Ramsgate beaches have steep stairs, others, such as Main Sands, provide accessible walkways and facilities. And, let's be honest, what's better than feeling sand between your toes and hearing waves gently break nearby?

Hidden Helpers

If you need help, don't be afraid to ask. Ramsgate residents are well-known for their friendliness—if you allow them, they'll talk to you for hours. Whether it's instructions or a recommendation for the best ice cream shop (hint: it's on the harbor), someone is always willing to help.

Getting to Ramsgate and navigating your way about is part of the trip. Whether you're speeding along the A299, seeing the countryside pass by from a train window, or simply strolling through the picturesque towns on foot, you'll find that the journey is as pleasurable as the destination.

So pack your luggage, charge your camera, and get ready for a memorable journey. Ramsgate is waiting to welcome you, and believe me, you'll adore being here.

HISTORY AND HERITAGE

Ramsgate is the type of town where history isn't just in the textbooks—it's in the air, the cobblestones, and the salty breeze that blows in from the sea. This town has a story to tell around every turn and believe me, it's worth listening to. Ramsgate's past feels alive, like a well-worn notebook filled with stories of bravery, camaraderie, and a splash of coastal mischief.

Ramsgate's Maritime Legacy

Let us begin with the obvious: Ramsgate is a beach town, and the water has been its lifeline for ages. Back then, Ramsgate's harbor was teeming with activity—ships coming and departing, fishermen hauling in their daily catch, and merchants negotiating over spices and silks.

But here's the truly fascinating part: Ramsgate isn't your average port. In 1821, King George IV granted it the official title of "Royal Harbour," making it the only one in England to do so. Why? Legend has it that George was so impressed by the hospitality he experienced here (and possibly the good gin) that he thought Ramsgate deserved some royal honor. Can you imagine the monarch raising a toast along the water's edge?

The harbor became a safe sanctuary for sailors traveling through the occasionally hazardous English Channel. During the Napoleonic Wars, it was essential, with vessels carrying troops and supplies passing through. Later, during World War II, Ramsgate stepped up once more, offering shelter to ships involved in the Dunkirk evacuation. Imagine hundreds of boats bobbing in the harbor, their crews gathering their breath before returning to danger.

Ramsgate's harbor protected not only ships but also stories.

Today, the Royal Harbour is a gorgeous center of activity, with colorful boats swaying gently and rigging clinking in the air. Grab a coffee from one of the quayside cafés, take a seat, and simply enjoy the scene. If you close your eyes, you can almost hear the echoes of the past—the creeks of timber ships, the shouting of dockworkers, and the call of gulls flying overhead.

Iconic Landmarks: The Royal Harbour and Beyond

The Royal Harbour

We've already discussed the harbor's royal status, but let's go a little further. The harbor's design is a masterpiece of Georgian engineering, with exquisite piers and curved stonework that has withstood the elements for generations. Walking down the East Pier will reward you with breathtaking views of the town, the coastline, and, on a clear day, even France (or so the locals claim—squint hard!).

However, the harbor is more than just a historical attraction. It's bustling with activity: fishing boats hauling in the day's catch, pleasure yachts drifting in, and a few seals popping up to say hello. Keep an eye out for the Sailor's Church, a small but noteworthy structure where sailors previously sought comfort and prayer.

Saint Augustine's Abbey and Shrine

A short stroll from the port leads to St. Augustine's Abbey, a Gothic Revival masterpiece constructed by Augustus Pugin. The monastery is an important element of Ramsgate's religious history, as it marks the location where St. Augustine came in AD 597 to spread Christianity throughout England.

Wander the gardens, see the beautiful brickwork, and take in the peaceful atmosphere of this sacred spot. Bonus points if you visit during one of the abbey's guided tours, which are jam-packed with intriguing details about Pugin's unusual life and the abbey's historical significance.

The Clock House

The Ramsgate Maritime Museum is housed in a 19th-century structure near the waterfront. Its famous clock tower serves as a sentinel, keeping time while you explore the museum's collections. Inside, you'll find displays about Ramsgate's shipwrecks, the fishing industry, and even the Dunkirk evacuation. It's a modest museum with a great heart, and it's the best place to learn more about the town's maritime history.

The Historic Tunnels of Ramsgate

If Ramsgate's waterfront depicts life on the surface, its network of underground tunnels depicts tenacity and survival. These tunnels, initially created to shelter villagers during WWII, are a fascinating piece of history lying beneath the surface.

During the Blitz, Ramsgate was a target for enemy bombers, therefore the residents sought a safe place to hide. Enter the Ramsgate Tunnels, a vast network of corridors dug into the chalky cliffs. At its peak, the tunnels stretched for four miles and could accommodate up to 60,000 people. Families dismantled furniture, put up kitchens, and even had communal gatherings underneath. Imagine living your daily life beneath the dirt as bombs rained down from above—a tribute to the town's tenacity and commitment.

Today, you can enjoy guided tours of the tunnels conducted by enthusiastic local historians who bring the past to life through stories of courage and humor. A guide told me of a woman who notoriously refused to evacuate without her piano. (Spoiler alert: she got it down there!) As you travel through the dimly lighted tunnels, you'll sense the weight of history about you. The subtle fragrance of damp chalk, the echoes of your footsteps—it's an experience that lingers long after you return to the sunlight.

Ramsgate's history is more than simply something you learn about; it's something you experience. From the majesty of the Royal Harbour to the quiet courage of the tunnels, every part of this town tells a story about the past. So take your time, let history wash over you, and let Ramsgate unveil itself layer by layer. Who knows. You might notice that the narrative of this coastal gem sounds a little like your own.

EXPLORING RAMSGATE'S COASTLINE

Ramsgate's coastline is a love letter from nature, with golden dunes, beautiful waves, and a few hidden gems just waiting for you to discover. Whether you're a beach bum, a hiker who enjoys panoramic vistas, or an adrenaline junkie ready to smash the surf, Ramsgate's coasts provide plenty to get your heart racing.

So grab your sun hat, walking shoes, or wetsuit (depending on your mood), and let's explore Ramsgate's coastal charms.

Top Beaches and Hidden Coves

When it comes to beaches, Ramsgate has you covered. There is a beach for everyone, no matter how big, little, sandy, or secluded.

Ramsgate Main Sands

Let's begin with the headliner of the show: Ramsgate Main Sands. This broad, sandy beach virtually begs you to take off your shoes and burrow your toes in. It's ideal for families and comes with everything you need, including lifeguards, beach cafés, and the iconic striped deckchairs.

On a bright day, you'll witness children constructing sandcastles, couples strolling hand in hand, and paddle boarders gliding serenely across the ocean. My advice? Head there early in the morning for a tranquil stroll while the sand is still chilly and the world is just waking up.

Western Undercliff Beach

If you like quieter, more rugged beaches, this is the place for you. Tucked behind the towering chalk cliffs, Western Undercliff feels like a secluded sanctuary. It is less busy than Main Sands, making it a favorite among residents. Furthermore, it's an excellent location for rock pooling—so channel your inner David Attenborough and see what you can find!

Hidden Coves

If you're the adventurous sort, Ramsgate's shoreline is littered with secluded coves that feel like they've come straight from a postcard. Pegwell Bay, for example, shows a large area of mudflats and salt marshes when the tide comes in. It's about exploring the unusual habitat, with birds flying overhead and the occasional seal lazing on the rocks, rather than swimming. Wear strong shoes—mudflats are aptly named "muddy"!

Coastal Walks with Stunning Views

If walking along the coast sounds like nirvana, Ramsgate will not disappoint. The area has some of the most stunning coastline walks in the UK, with pathways ranging from casual strolls to more difficult excursions.

The Viking Coast Trail

This 32-mile trail winds through Ramsgate, Broadstairs, Margate, and beyond, with sights that will make you halt in your tracks (and possibly reach for your camera). Don't worry, you don't have to accomplish everything at once. The Ramsgate-to-Broadstairs leg is particularly popular, taking you along cliff pathways with the sea on one side and rolling meadows on the other.

On my last trip here, I met a friendly local who claimed he had spotted a pod of dolphins from the cliffs the week before. While I didn't see any dolphins, I did witness a breathtaking sunset that felt like nature had turned the saturation up to the extreme.

Ramsgate Promenade

For something a little gentler on the legs, the Ramsgate Promenade is ideal. This flat, paved walk stretches beside the port and beach, providing views of both the water and the lively town. Stop for ice cream, relax on a bench, and simply watch the world go by—it's pure happiness.

The Pegwell Bay Walk

If you're looking for a more peaceful experience, the trek through Pegwell Bay Nature Reserve is a must. The walk meanders through salt marshes, dunes, and wildflower meadows, with the soothing sound of waves in the backdrop. Keep an eye out for wading birds and the occasional heron—this is a birdwatcher's dream.

Watersports and Boat Adventures

For those who can't resist the lure of the sea, Ramsgate's shoreline provides numerous options to get out on the water. Whether you're paddling, sailing, or plunging in headfirst (figuratively, please—always check the depth first!), an adventure awaits you.

Paddleboarding and Kayaking

Paddleboarding is considered a rite of passage in Ramsgate. There's nothing quite like floating down the quiet waters of the harbor, with the sun on your back and the occasional curious seal coming up to say hello. Kayaking is another excellent alternative for exploring the nooks and crannies of the shoreline that can only be reached by water.

Local firms provide rentals and instruction, so even if you've never done it before, you'll be an expert in no time. Just don't forget your sunscreen—a burnt paddleboarder does not look nice.

Sailing and Boating

If you've ever wanted to set sail, Ramsgate Port is the place to do it. Join a sailing tour to see the coastline from a different perspective, or rent a boat and set your course. Feeling fancy? Some tours even include champagne cruises at sunset. (Because nothing says "seaside luxury" like drinking champagne on a boat, right?)

Fishing Trips

Ramsgate has a variety of fishing charters available for individuals who enjoy fishing or simply want to pretend to be a rough fisherman for the day. Whether you're a seasoned angler or a complete beginner, there's something for you. If you're lucky, you may even catch your meal!

Ramsgate's coastline is an endless source of delight. From the golden beaches of Main beaches to the excitement of spotting animals at Pegwell Bay, from cliff-top walks to adrenaline-pumping watersports, there are plenty of reasons to fall in love with this length of England's coastline.

So what are you waiting for? Lace up your walking boots, grab your beach towel, and dust off your sailor's hat—it's time to discover Ramsgate's coastal gems. And who knows? You might even find a secret cove or two to call your own.

MUST-SEE ATTRACTIONS

Welcome to Ramsgate, where every corner appears to have a tale or a vista that will take your breath away. Ramsgate's attractions are numerous and delightful, ranging from historic sites steeped in history to museums filled with maritime tales.

Whether you're a history buff, an art lover, or simply someone who enjoys a good photo opportunity, these must-see locations will have you swooning and clicking pictures in no time.

Ramsgate Royal Harbour

Let us begin with Ramsgate's crowning achievement: the Royal Harbour. Imagine a lovely harbor lined with colorful boats bobbing softly on the ocean, surrounded by elegant Georgian architecture. It's the type of setting that makes you want to grab a coffee, sit on a sunny bench, and think you're in a love novel.

This isn't just any port; it's England's sole Royal Harbour, as designated by King George IV in 1821. (Apparently, the monarch enjoyed Ramsgate's hospitality; who wouldn't?) The port has witnessed it all: booming trade, fishing fleets, and even troops setting ships during the Napoleonic Wars. Today, it's a vibrant mix of recreational boats, working vessels, and charming cafés.

Stroll along the East Pier for breathtaking views of the coast, or visit the lively marina to watch the boats come and go. If you're lucky, you might even see a regatta or festival. Pro tip: go during sunset. Watching the sky become pink and gold over the sea is pure bliss.

Saint Augustine's Abbey and Shrine

A short stroll from the port leads to St. Augustine's Abbey and Shrine, a place of peaceful beauty and historical significance. This Gothic Revival masterpiece was created by Augustus Pugin, the same genius who designed the interiors of the Houses of Parliament.

The abbey is an homage to St. Augustine, the man credited with introducing Christianity to England. Legend has it that he landed around Ramsgate in AD 597, probably taking one look at the beach and saying, "Yep, this is the spot."

As you go around the grounds, you'll notice exquisite masonry, tranquil chapels, and plenty of places for solitary thought. There is also a small museum on site that explores the abbey's remarkable history. Even if you are not religious, there is something extremely compelling about standing in a location that has seen centuries of devotion.

Fun fact: *Augustus Pugin was quite the character. He once described his architectural style as "a good, solid, well-thought-out bit of medievalism." That's one way to describe it!*

Ramsgate Maritime Museum

The Ramsgate Maritime Museum offers a flavor of maritime nostalgia. This delightful museum, located in the ancient Clock House near the port, is a veritable treasure trove of nautical history.

The scent of salt air and the sound of seagulls outside will meet you as soon as you walk in, setting the tone for a deep dive into Ramsgate's naval history. The displays range from shipwrecks and smuggling to the town's involvement in the Dunkirk evacuation during World War II.

One of my favorite exhibitions is the collection of vintage navigation tools. Looking at them, you can't help but admire the bravery (and possibly lunacy) of sailors who ventured into the open sea with only a compass and a lot of hope. There's also an interesting display about the fishing industry, complete with historical images of fishermen who appear to be capable of arm wrestling a shark and winning.

Before you leave, make sure to take in the museum's renowned clock tower. It is an icon of Ramsgate and has been ticking for more than a century.

The Turner Contemporary

Okay, I understand what you're thinking: "Wait a minute, isn't that in Margate?" And technically, it is. But hear me out: The Turner Contemporary is less than a 15-minute drive from Ramsgate and well worth the little journey.

This modern art gallery, named after J.M.W. Turner, the famous landscape painter who was fascinated by the Kent coastline, stands as a beacon of innovation and culture. Turner once claimed that the sky over Thanet was "the loveliest in all Europe," and it's difficult to disagree when you're standing there, taking in the light and the scenery.

The gallery hosts a rotating lineup of modern art shows, so there is always something new to view. From thought-provoking installations to bright paintings, it's the type of place that makes you think, "I could be an artist...if only I had talent."

Even if modern art isn't your thing, the structure is worth seeing. Its clean architecture contrasts wonderfully with the craggy shoreline, and the huge windows provide stunning views of the sea. On a beautiful day, you might even see France on the horizon.

Make the most of your visit

Here's a recommendation for seeing Ramsgate's top attractions: take your time. These aren't simply bucket-list destinations; they're memorable experiences. Spend a leisurely afternoon touring the waterfront, relax in the abbey's gardens, and don't rush through the museum exhibits.

While you're at it, take time for the simple things, like a cup of tea at a comfortable café, a conversation with a friendly local, or a quiet moment watching the waves come in. Ramsgate has the ability to make you slow down and enjoy life's little pleasures.

So, whether you're learning about history at the abbey, digging into maritime stories, or being inspired at the Turner Contemporary, you're in for a treat. Ramsgate's attractions are more than just locations to see; they are stories to be uncovered. Go ahead and explore, allowing the town to captivate you. You will not regret it.

NATURE AND OUTDOORS

Ramsgate is more than simply picturesque harbors and historic landmarks; it is also a nature lover's paradise. With its breathtaking shoreline, calm parks, and rich animals, this seaside jewel provides countless opportunities to reconnect with nature. Whether you're wandering through a flower-filled garden, exploring an unspoiled nature reserve, or channeling your inner birdwatcher, Ramsgate is the ideal place to soak up nature's grandeur.

Pegwell Bay Nature Reserve

Let's start with Pegwell Bay, a natural wonder that feels like walking into another world. This large reserve, just a short distance from Ramsgate, is a nature lover's dream, with salt marshes, mudflats, and grassy cliffs to explore. It's the kind of setting where you feel like you've stepped into a BBC nature documentary—but without David Attenborough (unfortunately).

Pegwell Bay provides a haven for animals, particularly birds. During migration seasons, the mudflats become an avian airport, with wading species such as oystercatchers, curlews, and plovers landing to refuel. Grab your binoculars and see how many species you can spot—but be warned, the gulls may try to steal your meal if you aren't careful.

If birding isn't your thing, don't worry; there are lots of other activities to enjoy. The reserve's walking routes lead through stunning countryside, with views of the sea and the English Channel beyond. On a clear day, you may even see the faint silhouette of France in the distance. Pro tip: go during low tide when the mudflats are fully exposed and the harbor is bustling with activity.

One of my favorite memories from Pegwell Bay is coming across a small bunch of seals relaxing on the sandbanks. They appeared so comfortable that I nearly felt bad for disrupting their peace. (Don't worry—I stayed my distance; seals may be charming, but they have a bite to match!)

Parks, Gardens, and Open Spaces

When you're ready to switch from sea air to lush greenery, Ramsgate's parks and gardens have you covered. This community values its green spaces, so there are plenty of places to relax, picnic, or simply enjoy the landscape.

Ellington Park

Ellington Park is a popular neighborhood destination, and it's simple to understand why. With wide lawns, vivid flowerbeds, and even an antique bandstand, this park exudes old-fashioned charm. It's ideal for a relaxed afternoon; simply bring a blanket, a good book, and perhaps a sandwich or two.

If you're visiting during the summer, look for community events on the schedule. The park frequently accommodates outdoor concerts, craft fairs, and the occasional dog show. One year, I stumbled into a Victorian-themed picnic, replete with individuals dressed in historical costumes. (If you have never seen a man in a top hat eating a hot dog, you have not lived.)

King George VI Memorial Park

For something more formal, visit King George VI Memorial Park. This wonderfully maintained park features groomed gardens, tree-lined walks, and numerous benches where you can sit and observe the world go by. It also houses the Italianate Glasshouse, a beautiful 19th-century greenhouse stocked with exotic plants.

Because of the park's coastline location, you'll be treated to beautiful sea views—ideal for an early morning walk or a romantic sunset promenade. If you're traveling with children, the playground here is a huge hit.

Bird watching and Wildlife Spotting

Ramsgate's natural settings are not just gorgeous, but also abundant with animals. From fluttering butterflies to towering birds of prey, the town's diverse environments attract species of all sizes.

Bird Watching Highlights

Pegwell Bay is unquestionably the highlight of the show for birdwatchers, but it's not the only place to go. The cliffs along the Viking Coastal Trail are ideal for spotting kestrels, peregrine falcons, and even the occasional puffin. (Yes, puffins! They're elusive, so spotting one is a bonus.)

For a more relaxed bird watching experience, visit Monkton Nature Reserve. This quiet oasis is home to a variety of birds, as well as dragonfly and frog ponds. After a day of sightseeing, you can relax in the reserve's pleasant visitor center with a cup of tea.

Seal and Dolphin Spotting

If you're lucky, Ramsgate's seas may attract some larger creatures. Seals are a typical sight in Pegwell Bay, and they're always fun to watch as they laze on the sandbanks or swim gracefully through the waves.

Dolphins and porpoises occasionally appear along the coast. Keep a look out while wandering along the cliffs or enjoying a boat ride; you never know when one of these playful creatures will come up to say hello.

Making the most of Ramsgate's outdoor spaces

Exploring Ramsgate's natural beauty is more than just seeing the sights; it's about having an experience. Whether you're trekking along a cliffside route, picnicking in a flower-filled park, or just observing birds at daybreak, there's a sense of peace and connection that's difficult to describe.

And let's be honest: nature in Ramsgate has a way of surprising you. One moment you're admiring a wildflower meadow, the next you're being duped by a very cunning seagull. (Seriously, they have no shame; protect your chips with your life.

So, lace up your walking boots, bring your binoculars, and prepare to be enchanted. Ramsgate's outdoor spaces are more than just places to visit; they are places to fall in love with. And who knows? You could even find yourself humming a melody as you walk along Pegwell Bay, channeling your inner nature documentary host. "And here, in the wilds of Ramsgate..."

FOOD AND DRINK

Ramsgate is more than just a visual feast; it's also a culinary delight. From traditional Kentish pleasures to fashionable beachfront cafés, the town provides a culinary excursion as vivid and diverse as its coastline. Whether you enjoy seafood, pubs, or exquisite cuisine, Ramsgate has something for you.

Traditional Kentish Cuisine

When visiting Ramsgate, eating like a native is essential. Kent, sometimes known as the "Garden of England," is well known for its fresh fruit, which shines through in traditional recipes.

Seafood, Fresh from the Water

Let's start with the obvious: Ramsgate's seafood scene is strong. As a coastal town, it's no wonder that the native cuisine focuses on the catch of the day. Consider delicious oysters, plump mussels, and flaky Dover soles. If you haven't experienced Whitstable oysters (a Kentish specialty), Ramsgate is the ideal place to do so.

During my last visit, I ordered a dish of fish and chips from a small harborside restaurant. The fish was so fresh that it almost jumped off the dish, and the chips were golden perfection. A seagull attempted to swipe one, but I couldn't blame it.

Kentish Classics

Beyond seafood, don't overlook foods that reflect Kent's agricultural bounty. Look for traditional dishes like lamb with mint sauce from Romney Marsh's verdant pastures, as well as fruity sweets like cherry pie and apple crumble. Combine these with a drink of Kentish cider or ale for the ultimate local experience.

Best Seafront Cafés and Pubs

Ramsgate's seafront is surrounded by quaint cafés and vibrant bars where you may dine with a view of the surf. These restaurants are about more than just fantastic food; they're also about the atmosphere.

Harbor View Cafe

This beautiful café is right on the edge of Ramsgate's Royal Harbour, offering breathtaking views as well as a menu of hearty breakfasts and light lunches. There's something beautiful about sipping a latte and watching the boats bobble in the marina. Their crab sandwiches are a local favorite, and for good reason: they're full of flavor with just the right amount of mayo.

The Churchill Tavern

If you want a traditional British pub experience, The Churchill Tavern is the place to go. Nestled on the West Cliff, this bar mixes ancient charm with breathtaking views. Their Sunday roast is legendary, featuring fluffy Yorkshire puddings and award-winning gravy. I once spent an entire afternoon here, sipping a pint of local ale and debating whether the sea or the roast potatoes were more appealing. (Spoiler: it was tied.)

The Lookout Cafe

The Lookout Café offers a more calm atmosphere. Perched on a rock overlooking the beach, it's the perfect place for brunch or afternoon tea. Their scones with clotted cream and jam are the stuff of dreams, but make sure to reserve room for the handmade desserts!

Top-Rated Restaurants for Every Budget

Ramsgate's restaurant scene caters to all tastes and budgets, from casual to upscale dining. Whatever your appetite is, you'll find a place that will satisfy it.

Budget-Friendly Bites

If you're traveling on a budget, don't worry—Ramsgate has plenty of economical yet delicious options.

- **Peter's Fish Factory:** A no-frills chippy near the sea that delivers some of the greatest fish and chips around. Grab a takeaway and eat it on the beach to complete the coastal experience.

- **Flavors by Kumar:** This family-run Indian restaurant is a hidden gem, serving delicious curries at affordable prices. Their butter chicken is the perfect comfort food.

Mid-Range Marvels

Looking for a sit-down supper that won't break the bank? These mid-range positions are bound to impress:

- **The Royal Victoria Pavilion:** A beautiful Wetherspoon bar located in a historic pavilion, is worth visiting for its architecture alone. The meal is reasonably priced, and the views are magnificent.

- **A La Turka Ramsgate:** Specializes in Turkish cuisine, serving sizzling kebabs, fresh salads, and mezze platters that are ideal for sharing. The pleasant, inviting atmosphere is simply the cherry on top.

Fine Dining and Special Occasions

When it comes to treating yourself, Ramsgate boasts some very great fine dining options:

- **Albion House Hotel Restaurant:** This magnificent restaurant overlooks the bay and serves exquisite cuisine made with locally produced ingredients. Their tasting menu takes you on an unforgettable culinary adventure.

- **Bon Appetit:** This French-themed bistro is ideal for a romantic evening. The intimate atmosphere, great service, and beautifully prepared dishes make each dinner feel like a celebration.

Local Markets and Food Festivals

Don't miss Ramsgate's local markets and food festivals, where you can try fresh fruit, artisanal cheeses, baked products, and more. The town's weekly market is an excellent spot to grab a quick lunch or get mementos for the foodies in your life.

If you visit during the summer, the annual Ramsgate Festival frequently includes a food fair with stalls selling everything from Kentish wines to homemade fudge. My advice? Go hungry—you'll want to sample everything.

A *Culinary Adventure awaits*

Ramsgate's food scene is a delectable blend of traditional flavors and modern ingenuity, all presented with a touch of seaside charm. Every bite tells a tale, whether you're eating fish and chips by the waterfront or sitting down to a multi-course meal in a fine dining establishment.

So, loosen your belt, pack your appetite, and prepare to eat your way around Ramsgate. Just keep an eye out for those cheeky seagulls—they aren't bashful about joining the feast!

SHOPPING IN RAMSGATE

If Ramsgate's stunning views and ancient charm don't entice you, its shopping district may be. This coastal town boasts an eclectic mix of artisan stores, quirky boutiques, and bustling markets, making it a shoppers' paradise.

Whether you're looking for the ideal souvenir, one-of-a-kind gifts, or something to spoil yourself, Ramsgate provides a lovely shopping experience with plenty of surprises along the way.

Artisan Shops and Boutiques

Let's begin with Ramsgate's artisan shops and boutiques—the kind of places where you feel like you've discovered hidden treasures. These aren't your standard high-street boutiques; they're full of personality, enthusiasm, and unique products.

Nice things

Essentially, the name says it all. This independent boutique, located in the heart of Ramsgate, is a refuge for handcrafted, locally sourced items. Every item in the store, from finely created ceramics to one-of-a-kind jewelry, tells a story.

I once spent a half-hour talking with the owner about a set of hand-painted mugs, only to leave with a scarf that I didn't realize I wanted but now can't live without.

The Little Bazaar

Stepping into The Little Bazaar immerses you in a world of bohemian charm. This store focuses on ethical and sustainable products, including creative apparel and one-of-a-kind homeware. If you enjoy discovering something unique, here is the place for you.

Bonus: the staff is so pleasant that they will likely remember your name the next time you visit.

Vinyl Head

Music lovers rejoice! Vinyl Head is an independent record store with an extensive collection of new and antique vinyl. Whether you enjoy rock, jazz, or something more obscure, you're sure to find a treasure to add to your collection. Additionally, the intimate atmosphere and occasional live music events make it a must-see for audiophiles.

Local Markets and Souvenirs

No vacation to Ramsgate is complete without visiting the markets. These lively spaces are full of charm, selling everything from fresh fruit to homemade items.

Ramsgate Market

Ramsgate Market, held weekly in the town center, is a lively event including everything from artisanal breads and cheeses to vintage apparel and antiques. It's the ideal spot to soak up the local atmosphere while browsing stalls run by enthusiastic sellers.

Pro tip: *arrive early to get the greatest deals, and don't forget to try the freshly made pastries—they're worth the trip alone.*

Made in the Thanet Market

If you're visiting on the first Saturday of the month, stop by the Made in Thanet Market. This pop-up market honors local creatives by featuring homemade items such as artwork, candles, and unique home décor.

The last time I went, I bought a watercolor print of Ramsgate's Royal Harbour, which now hangs proudly in my living room.

Harbor stalls

For something more casual, visit the little kiosks lining the port. These are ideal for purchasing beach-themed souvenirs such as shell jewelry, homemade soaps, and cute trinkets for friends and family back home. And let's be honest: you can never have enough boat-shaped fridge magnets.

Tips for Unique Finds

Shopping in Ramsgate is more than just what you buy; it's about the experience. Here are some suggestions to help you discover the town's best-kept retail secrets:

Explore the side streets

While Ramsgate's main shopping areas are fantastic, some of the most lovely businesses are hidden away down quiet side lanes. Don't be scared to travel; you never know what hidden gems you'll discover.

Chat with the locals

Speaking with locals is one of the finest ways to uncover interesting areas. Shop proprietors and market vendors are frequently delighted to provide recommendations for other locations to explore. As a bonus, you may learn about local history or hear a hilarious anecdote.

Embrace the unexpected

Some of the best findings occur when you aren't hunting for anything specific. Keep an open mind, and you might just come away with a new favorite piece of art, a unique antique, or the ideal pair of earrings.

Support local creators

Ramsgate is home to many outstanding artisans and makers, so try to shop locally wherever possible. Not only will you take home something incredibly unique, but you will also be helping the community. It's a win-win!

Make the Most of Your Shopping Spree

Shopping in Ramsgate is more than a transaction; it's an adventure. Whether you're wandering around the market, visiting a boutique, or chatting with a vendor, each experience enhances the allure of discovering this seaside town.

And let us not overlook the pleasure of people-watching. One of my favorite things to do is grab a coffee, sit in a sunny area near the port, and watch the world go by. It's so satisfying to watch Ramsgate's magic being discovered one shop at a time by both locals and visitors.

So take your tote bag, put on your most comfy shoes, and prepare to shop till you drop (or run out of pounds). Ramsgate's distinct blend of artisan charm and seaside character will undoubtedly leave you with a few treasures—and perhaps a humorous story or two—to bring home.

Oh, and one more thing: if you notice a seagull eyeing your munchies while you're admiring your purchases, guard them at all means. These cheeky birds are expert opportunists.

FESTIVALS AND EVENTS

Ramsgate may be a quiet seaside town most of the time, but when it comes to festivals and events, it knows how to party! Ramsgate hosts a diverse range of celebrations throughout the year, from food fairs to music festivals that will make your heart skip a beat.

Whether you're traveling for a weekend or staying for an extended period, there's always something going on to make your experience even more magical.

Annual Highlights: From Food Fairs to Music Festivals

Ramsgate's calendar is jam-packed with annual events celebrating its culture, community, and creativity. Here are some highlights you shouldn't miss:

Ramsgate Festival of Sound

This colorful music and arts event is one of the town's highlights. Typically held in late summer, the Ramsgate Festival of Sound transforms the town into a massive stage, with performances ranging from live bands to spoken word and everything in between.

I once came across a pop-up jazz band performing in the center of the Royal Harbour, and it was pure bliss. Imagine standing under the sunset, a nice sea breeze on your face, and a saxophone serenading you—it's an experience you'll remember forever.

Ramsgate Food Festival

Calling all foodies! This annual event celebrates Kent's gastronomic heritage, with everything from fresh seafood to artisanal cheeses and craft breweries. Wander around kiosks stacked high with local goods, watch live cooking demos, and, most importantly, enjoy all of the free samples.

One year, I came across a kiosk selling lavender-infused fudge. It sounded strange but tasted delicious. It's now my go-to "unique gift" for friends back home (and sometimes for myself).

Thanet Pride

Ramsgate radiates with love and inclusivity during Thanet Pride, the LGBTQ+ community's annual festival. Expect dazzling parades, live performances, and a festive mood that spreads across the town. Rainbows, laughing, and enough glitter to make a mermaid jealous are the highlights of this day.

Seasonal Events in 2025

There is always something spectacular going on in Ramsgate, regardless of the time of year. Here's a seasonal guide to what's happening in 2025:

Spring

Spring in Ramsgate is all about new beginnings and blossoming beauty.

- **Easter Harbour Fair:** Held throughout the Easter weekend, this family-friendly event includes market vendors, live entertainment, and children's activities such as egg hunts and face painting.

- **Coastal Clean-Up Days:** Join the community in giving back to nature by volunteering at one of the town's beach cleanup programs. It's an excellent chance to meet new people while also enjoying the fresh spring air.

Summer

Summer is when Ramsgate comes to life.

- **Viking Bay Regatta:** Located in nearby Broadstairs, this event is well worth the short drive. Watch colorful boats race along the coast while enjoying live music and food stalls.

- **Open-Air Cinema Nights:** Bring a blanket and watch great flicks under the stars in Ellington Park. (Hint: Bring munchies, but watch out for those annoying seagulls!)

Autumn

Ramsgate continues to celebrate as the leaves turn golden.

- **Harvest Festival at St. George's Church:** A traditional seasonal festival featuring local produce displays and a welcoming community atmosphere.

- **Oktoberfest Ramsgate:** Dress in lederhosen and raise a stein at this boisterous beer festival. Expect German-inspired cuisine, live music, and enough pretzels to last until Christmas.

Winter

Winter in Ramsgate is comfortable, lively, and cheerful.

- **Christmas Lantern Parade:** Watch the town light up as citizens parade through the streets carrying wonderfully carved lanterns. The parade concludes at the port when the Christmas lights are turned on for a spectacular display.

- **New Year's Eve Fireworks:** Bring in 2026 with a boom as fireworks illuminate the sky over the Royal Harbour. Pro tip: find a place early—it gets busy!

Cultural Celebrations

Ramsgate's rich history and diverse culture mean there are plenty of cultural events to enjoy.

Saint Augustine's Feast Day

This yearly ceremony commemorates St. Augustine, the man who introduced Christianity to England. The celebration, held at St. Augustine's Shrine, will feature special liturgies, historical reenactments, and traditional music. Even if you aren't religious, the pageantry and history are intriguing to watch.

Ramsgate Carnival

Ramsgate Carnival, which dates back to the early twentieth century, is a popular annual event that draws visitors from all across Kent. Floats, dancers, and costumed performers parade through the streets, producing a vibrant sight that is impossible not to smile at.

Heritage Open Days

Ramsgate's historic buildings are available to the public every September as part of Heritage Available Days. It's a unique opportunity to discover hidden jewels such as private residences, old churches, and even subterranean tunnels.

Last year, I explored a 19th-century mansion that still had its original wallpaper—it was like going back in time.

Tips to Enjoy Ramsgate's Events

- **Plan Ahead:** Some events, like the Ramsgate Festival of Sound, are quite popular and might become overcrowded. To minimize disappointment, book your tickets and lodgings early.

- **Dress for the weather:** Because Ramsgate is located on the shore, the weather can change quickly. Bring layers, a raincoat, and comfortable shoes; you'll thank me later.

- **Get Involved:** Many events provide options for guests to engage, such as attending a workshop, volunteering, or dancing in a parade. Don't be shy—jump in and create some memories!

Ramsgate's festivals and events are more than simply a fun time; they celebrate everything that makes our town unique. Whether you're dancing to live music, enjoying a local delicacy, or watching fireworks light up the waterfront, you'll depart with a smile and memories to tell.

So mark your calendar, pack your party hat, and get ready to have some fun. Every day in Ramsgate feels like a festival!

DAY TRIP AND EXCURSION

While Ramsgate is a treasure in its own right, its position makes it an ideal starting point for discovering more of Kent's gems. From picturesque coastal villages to lush countryside and historic cities, there's a lot to see and do right nearby. Grab your daypack and let's go on some amazing day trips and excursions!

Nearby Coastal Towns: Broadstairs and Margate

If you think Ramsgate's shoreline is lovely (and it is), wait till you see its delightful neighbors, Broadstairs and Margate. These two seaside communities are full of character, each with its distinct flavor of coastal romance.

Broadstairs: The Charming and Cozy Seaside Escape

Broadstairs is either a 10-minute drive or a short train trip from Ramsgate and feels like walking into a postcard. Known for its Dickensian charm (yep, Charles Dickens was a fan), this town has golden beaches, eccentric boutiques, and a timeless atmosphere.

Begin your vacation with Viking Bay, a crescent-shaped beach ideal for sunbathing, canoeing, or simply relaxing on a bench with a tub of fresh local ice cream. I spent an afternoon here with a book and just read one phrase since the scenery kept distracting me.

If you enjoy literature, don't miss Bleak House, where Dickens wrote parts of David Copperfield. You can take a tour or simply enjoy the building from the outside, believing you're an extra in a period drama.

Margate: The Trendy and Artsy Neighbor

Margate, located a little farther up the coast, has seen a significant transformation in recent years. It's a paradise for artists, foodies, and everyone who enjoys a blend of retro ambiance and contemporary ingenuity.

Art aficionados should visit the Turner Contemporary, a spectacular exhibition inspired by the work of J.M.W. Turner, who once painted the sky above Margate. Even if modern art isn't to your taste, the views from the gallery are worth seeing.

For some fun, visit Dreamland, a vintage-style amusement park with antique rides, live music, and more candy floss than you can handle.

I once attempted the dodgems here and laughed so hard that I almost fell out of the car.

Exploring Kent's Countryside

For those who crave greenery and rolling hills, Kent's countryside is nothing short of perfect. It's no surprise that this region is dubbed the "Garden of England."

Richborough Roman Fort

A short journey from Ramsgate will take you to the remnants of Richborough Roman Fort, one of Britain's most significant Roman sites. Walking among the ancient ruins, you can almost hear the footsteps of Roman soldiers and traders that came through this entrance to Britannia.

Bring a picnic and take your time enjoying the calm surroundings. Just keep an eye out for the occasional sheep—their stare makes you wonder if they're secretly critiquing your sandwich choice.

The Kent Downs

For true nature lovers, the Kent Downs Area of Outstanding Natural Beauty is a must-see. With its undulating hills, small villages, and winding footpaths, this is the countryside at its best.

One of my favorite walks begins in Wye and leads up to the Devil's Kneading Trough, a breathtaking natural amphitheater. The vistas from the top are well worth the effort—just don't forget your camera (or your breath; the hike is steep!).

Historic Canterbury

No journey to Kent is complete without a visit to Canterbury, a city rich in history and brimming with charm. It's only a 30-minute train ride from Ramsgate, making it the ideal destination for a day filled with culture, history, and whimsy.

Canterbury Cathedral

Let us begin with the star of the show: Canterbury Cathedral, a UNESCO World Heritage Site, and the seat of the Archbishop of Canterbury. This magnificent structure, which has stood for more than 1,400 years, is a Gothic architectural masterpiece.

Take a tour to learn about its intriguing history, which includes the notorious murder of Archbishop Thomas Becket in 1170. Standing in the precise location where it occurred gave me goosebumps—and not only because the cathedral is a touch drafty.

Strolling Through The City

After exploring the church, go through Canterbury's cobblestone streets. The city is brimming with independent stores, quiet cafés, and riverbank walks. I highly recommend going on a punting tour down the River Stour. Gliding through the river while your guide tells you local stories is the epitome of calm.

The Canterbury Tales Experience

If you're a fan of literature or simply appreciate a good narrative, visit the Canterbury Tales Experience. It's a fun and participatory way to see Chaucer's medieval classic, filled with costumed characters and plenty of laughs.

Tips for Day Trips

Plan Your Transportation

Kent is well-connected by trains, buses, and attractive driving roads, making it simple to navigate. If you're visiting numerous sites in one day, consider purchasing a day travel pass—it's inexpensive and hassle-free.

Pack for All Weathers

Kent's weather is unpredictable, so bring clothes, a raincoat, and comfortable walking shoes. There's nothing worse than having soaked socks midway through a country stroll.

Bring snacks

While there are lots of places to eat, it's always a good idea to bring some snacks. I once miscalculated how long a country walk would take and ended up sharing my emergency granola bar with a tenacious duck.

Take It Slow

Day trips are about exploring and enjoying, not rushing. Choose one or two destinations per day to truly enjoy the experience.

Ramsgate's surroundings provide numerous options for adventure, ranging from sandy beaches to undulating hills and historic landmarks. Whether you're drinking up Margate's artistic vitality, discovering the quiet Kent Downs, or walking in the footsteps of pilgrims in Canterbury, each day trip adds a new depth to your Kentish adventure.

So, take your map (or GPS), lace up your shoes, and prepare to discover the best of Ramsgate's neighbors. Adventure is right around the corner—sometimes literally!

WHERE TO STAY

So, you've decided to explore Ramsgate—great decision! But, before you start arranging your agenda, consider where you'll sleep after a long day of beach activities. Ramsgate has a wide range of hotels, from luxurious resorts with harbor views to tiny, budget-friendly hideaways. Whatever your vacation style, there's an ideal location for you.

Luxury Hotels and Boutique Stays

Ramsgate's finest accommodations provide comfort, style, and, in many cases, a stunning view of the sea.

Albion House Hotel

If you're searching for a destination with history and charm, Albion House Hotel is the crown jewel of Ramsgate's upscale scene.

This Georgian beauty overlooks the Royal Harbour and features exquisite suites, sumptuous furnishings, and service that will make you feel like royalty.

The on-site restaurant is delightful, serving fresh, locally sourced cuisine. I once had their scallop starter and almost ordered it twice—who needs a main course when perfection is presented on a little plate?

The Royal Harbor Hotel

This boutique find is a lovely blend of classic and whimsical. The Royal Harbour Hotel, located just a short walk from the town center, is recognized for its eclectic décor, which includes antiques, artwork, and comfortable fireplaces perfect for curling up with a book.

Oh, and breakfast? Imagine yourself eating a substantial English meal while watching boats bobbing in the harbor. It is the kind of start to the day that makes you think, "I could get used to this life."

Family Friendly Accommodations

Traveling with children? Not a problem! Ramsgate offers a variety of options to keep the entire family comfortable and entertained.

Premier Inn Ramsgate (Manston airport)

The Premier Inn Ramsgate is a simple, dependable alternative for families, with big rooms, comfortable beds, and a restaurant serving kid-friendly dishes (hello, chicken nuggets). It's also an ideal location for exploring Ramsgate and the surrounding area.

Holiday parks and self-catering homes

Ramsgate's holiday parks and self-catering villas are ideal for families that require more room (and perhaps a kitchen to prepare those critical snack breaks).

One popular option is Two Chimneys Holiday Park, which is located just outside town. It has a pool, playgrounds, and plenty of open space for children to play while parents relax with a cup of tea—or a cheeky glass of wine.

Budget-Friendly Options and Hostels

If you're traveling on a tight budget, don't worry—Ramsgate has plenty of inexpensive options that don't sacrifice comfort or character.

Travelodge Ramsgate

You know what you're getting with a Travelodge: clean, efficient rooms at affordable costs. Located on the outskirts of Ramsgate, it's an excellent starting point for visiting the town without breaking the bank. In addition, there is free parking, which is a great plus if you're driving through Kent.

Hostels and Guesthouses

Ramsgate's hostels and guesthouses are ideal for single travelers and those wishing to meet new people.

Ramsgate Backpackers Hostel is a pleasant hostel with dormitory-style rooms and a shared kitchen. It's simple, but the friendly environment and central location make it a popular choice among budget-conscious travelers.

Pro tip: *Book early during the summer months, since these places tend to fill rapidly. Ramsgate's prominence as a coastal destination means that even low-cost solutions are in high demand.*

Which Neighborhood Is Right For You?

Choosing the proper place to stay can make all the difference. Here is a basic breakdown:

- **Harbor & Seafront:** Ideal for people who want to be at the center of the action. This region is perfect for convenient access to restaurants, stores, and the stunning views of the Royal Harbour.

- **East Cliff:** East Cliff is quieter and more residential, with nice bed and breakfasts and a serene environment. It's ideal for families or anyone wanting a more relaxed atmosphere.

- **Outskirts of Ramsgate**: Budget visitors and road trippers will appreciate the convenience and affordability of motels on Ramsgate's outskirts. While you will need transportation to reach the main sites, it is an excellent way to save money.

Tips for Choosing the Perfect Stay

- **Book early:** Ramsgate is a popular destination, particularly during the summer and festival season. Secure your position early to prevent missing out on your first pick.

- **Check Reviews:** While most accommodations in Ramsgate are excellent, it's always a good idea to examine reviews on sites such as TripAdvisor or Booking.com to verify you're making the best decision.

- **Consider Amenities:** Determine what is important to you. Free Wi-Fi? On-site parking? A killer breakfast spread? Check that your accommodations meet all of the requirements.

- **Investigate Self-Catering Options:** If you're staying for more than a few days, consider renting a vacation house or apartment. It allows you the freedom to prepare your meals and feel more at home.

A Home away from Home

Ramsgate's accommodations cater to everyone, whether you choose to stay in a beautiful boutique hotel or a low-cost hostel. What distinguishes this town is the warmth and generosity you will encounter wherever you visit.

I will never forget my first trip to Ramsgate. I stayed at a modest guesthouse run by a retired couple who welcomed me like family. They insisted I eat their handmade marmalade for breakfast, and years later, I still dream about it. Ramsgate has a way of making you feel like you belong—and that sensation usually begins with where you stay.

So, choose your ideal location, unpack your baggage, and prepare to create some great moments. Whether you wake up to a view of the harbor, sip tea in a charming B&B, or share stories in a hostel common room, one thing is certain: Ramsgate will seem like a home away from home.

PLANNING YOUR VISIT

So, you intend to visit Ramsgate? A fantastic decision! Whether you're looking for sunny beach days, gorgeous coastal hikes, or comfortable winter evenings by the sea, Ramsgate provides something for you all year. To help you make the most of your stay, we'll go over the when, what, and how of arranging your Ramsgate adventure.

Best Time to Visit Ramsgate

Ramsgate is open year-round, although your experience will change according to the season. Here's what each one offers:

Spring (March-May): A Blooming Delight

Spring in Ramsgate is like seeing a pastel painting come to life. The gardens are filled with blooms, and the beach walkways are sprinkled with colorful daffodils. The weather is pleasant, making it ideal for walking excursions and enjoying the town's outdoor attractions away from the summer throng.

One spring, I packed a picnic and went to Pegwell Bay Nature Reserve. Between the chirping birds and the refreshing sea wind, it felt as if nature was putting on a special performance just for me.

Pro tip: *bring a light jacket because the breeze can still be cold.*

Summer (June–August): Beach Bliss

Summer is Ramsgate's peak season and with good cause. The town is alive with activity as locals and visitors swarm to the sandy beaches. The Royal Harbour is bustling with yachts, and outdoor eating options are in full flow.

If you visit around this period, you may expect to see a variety of events, including food festivals and outdoor performances. Just be prepared for crowds—Viking Bay and Ramsgate Main Sands are popular, so arrive early to secure your preferred beach location.

Autumn (September-November): A Cozy Escape

Autumn in Ramsgate is an underappreciated masterpiece. The summer throngs have left, although the weather frequently remains nice well into October. It's the best time for individuals who enjoy lengthy seaside walks and breathtaking sunsets.

During one of my autumn visits, I discovered a small market selling homemade products and seasonal delights. I ended up purchasing a wool scarf, which is now my "Ramsgate souvenir"—and a perfect motivation to return during the cooler months.

Winter (December–February): Quiet Charm

In the winter, Ramsgate offers a pleasant, almost romantic ambiance. The town slows down, making it ideal for a quiet escape. Imagine sitting at a seaside café, sipping hot chocolate, and watching the waves crash on the coast.

If you're lucky, you might see the yearly Christmas lights illuminating the Royal Harbour—it's a scene straight out of a holiday movie. Simply bundle up; the breeze from the water might be brisk!

Packing Essentials for Every Season

Packing for Ramsgate is all about preparedness. Here's a fast guide to ensure you're protected:

Spring

- Layers! The weather can quickly flip from sunny to frigid.

- A lightweight raincoat—because this is England.

- Comfortable walking shoes for exploring gardens and seaside trails.

Summer

- Sunscreen and a sun hat. Ramsgate may not be tropical, but the sun can still sneak up on you.

- A beach bag including towels, swimwear, and flip-flops.

- A light cardigan or jacket for chilly evenings.

Autumn

- A comfortable sweater or two for the cool coastal breezes.

- A thermos for warm drinks on walks.

- Autumn showers do exist, so wear waterproof shoes.

Winter

- A cozy coat, scarf, hat, and gloves. Ramsgate's wind might feel like it's throwing you an enthusiastic high-five in the face.

- Boots with a strong grip for cold mornings.

- A good book for a cozy evening.

- Don't forget your camera, regardless of the season! Ramsgate's scenery is always Instagrammable.

Tips for Sustainable Travel

Traveling wisely does not have to mean giving up enjoyment. Sustainable choices frequently result in more real experiences. Here's how to leave a light footprint while visiting Ramsgate:

Choose Eco-Friendly Transportation

Ramsgate is well-connected by public transport, so avoid driving if possible. To visit surrounding towns such as Broadstairs and Margate, take the train from London or a local bus. Walking or cycling are the most efficient ways to move around Ramsgate.

On my last trip, I rented a bike and spent the day riding the Viking Coastal Trail. Not only was it environmentally responsible, but it also allowed me to stop whenever I wanted to observe the scenery (and have some fish & chips).

Support local businesses

Ramsgate thrives on its local economy, which includes artisan stores and family-run restaurants. Avoid the huge chains and spend your money where it matters. Trust me, the hand-thrown clay mug you purchase from a local artist will store both your morning coffee and your journey memories.

Be mindful of wildlife

If you're visiting Pegwell Bay or other natural areas, stick to the approved routes and stay away from wildlife. Feeding seagulls may appear sweet at first, but trust me—they do not respect boundaries and will follow you around for the rest of the day like feathered paparazzi.

Reduce waste

Pack a reusable water bottle and shopping bag. Many local businesses are eager to refill your bottle, and you'll avoid contributing to single-use plastic garbage.

Respect the locals

This may seem apparent, but it is worth stating. Ramsgate is both a working town and a tourist destination, so be mindful of its citizens. A grin and a friendly "hello" go a long way in this situation.

A Trip worth Planning

Planning a trip to Ramsgate is part of the adventure. Every detail adds to the enjoyment, whether you're planning a trip to attend a summer festival, packing layers for a springtime beach walk, or deciding on the most sustainable options.

Ramsgate has a way of making tourists feel like old friends. From its sunny beaches to its warm winter charm, each season brings a new reason to fall in love with this coastal gem. So pack your bags (and your sense of adventure) and prepare to create wonderful experiences.

Trust me, Ramsgate is worth every checklist, raincoat, and planning time. Let's get this trip started!

LOCAL INSIGHTS AND TIPS

So you've made it to Ramsgate—great choice! This picturesque coastal town has so much to offer, and with a few insider advice, you'll fit in like a local while avoiding the traps of the unprepared visitor. Are you ready to unveil Ramsgate's secrets? Let's plunge in!

Common Phrases and Local Etiquette

First and foremost, because Ramsgate is in England, there may be certain linguistic and behavioral differences to be aware of.

"Kentish" contrasts with "Kentish Man/Woman"

Kent residents are extremely proud of their ancestry. You may hear the terms "Kentish Man" or "Man of Kent," which have historically been used to refer to people from different parts of Kent. Don't worry; Ramsgate residents are generally laid-back, so you won't need a geography degree to make friends!

Polite greetings

The British are known for their politeness, and Ramsgate is no exception. A pleasant "hello" or "good morning" is always received with a smile. Bonus points if you make a friendly weather comment—"It's a beautiful day, isn't it?" works even when it is raining.

Queueing Culture

Let's discuss the art of the queue (line). Ramsgate residents enjoy an orderly queue, whether for ice cream, the bus, or a space at the fishmonger's counter. Cutting in line is completely unacceptable. Be patient, and you will fit right in.

Avoiding Tourist Traps

Even in a charming town like Ramsgate, there are a few traps to avoid to enhance your experience.

Overpriced seafront cafés

While the seaside has many fantastic restaurants, some cater to tourists rather than locals, resulting in higher pricing and occasionally lesser quality. If a menu has fuzzy food photographs, you should probably move away.

Instead, go slightly off the beaten route to places like The Goose or Archive Coffee, where you'll get great food and drinks without the tourist price tag.

"Authentic" souvenirs

Avoid cheap magnets and "I ♥ Ramsgate" mugs manufactured in another country. Instead, purchase at local artisan stores for handmade items such as pottery, jewelry, or even a jar of locally sourced jam. Nice Things Ramsgate is a treasure trove of interesting things.

Paying too much for tours

While guided excursions can be enjoyable, Ramsgate's allure lies in its walkability. Get a map, or better yet, ask a local for suggestions. You'll save money and most likely find hidden gems along the road.

Insider Recommendations

Now for the juicy part: Ramsgate's best-kept secrets, which only locals (and now you) are aware of.

The best place for a sunrise

If you're an early riser, come to East Cliff Promenade for the best sunrise views across the ocean. Bring a coffee and a thick coat, and watch as the first rays of light illuminate the Royal Harbour in golden hues. I promise it's worth the early alarm.

Hidden Foodie Gem

While everyone raves about the fish and chips (and they should—try Peter's Fish Factory), locals know that Baked by the Sea has the tastiest sandwiches in town. Their sourdough masterpieces are legendary. What about the pulled pork sandwich? Life-changing.

Quiet Beach Escape

Main Sands receives all of the attention, but if you prefer a more tranquil location, go to Dumpton Gap. It's a short walk from the main stretch and seems like your own personal beach, especially at low tide.

Local Pub Scene

For a pint with personality, avoid the commercial pubs and go to The Artillery Arms. It's modest, intimate, and full of friendly locals who are eager to provide tips or simply discuss Ramsgate's history over a beer.

Emergency Contacts and Useful Numbers

While we hope your trip goes smoothly, it is always a good idea to be prepared. Here's a short reference for key contacts in Ramsgate:

- **Emergency services (police, fire, ambulance):** Dial 999 for immediate assistance.

- **Non-emergency police:** Call 101 for less urgent problems, such as reporting lost things.

- **Local Hospital (QEQM Hospital, Margate):** 01843 225544. This is the closest hospital with an Accident and Emergency (A&E) department.

- **Pharmacies:** Boots in the town center (01843 592020) is a dependable source for over-the-counter medications and prescriptions.

- **Tourist Information:** For assistance, please visit the Ramsgate Visitor Information Centre or contact 01843 577577.

- **Taxi Services:** Central Cars Ramsgate (01843 888888) provides dependable local transportation.

- **Lost and Found:** Did you misplace something? Visit the Ramsgate Police Station or check with neighboring businesses. Ramsgate residents are generous and frequently go out of their way to reconcile people with misplaced belongings.

Navigating Ramsgate like a native requires only a pinch of curiosity, a dash of sociability, and perhaps a little tolerance for the occasional queue. Avoid tourist traps, embrace local eccentricities, and do not be hesitant to ask for recommendations. Ramsgate is a town that enjoys sharing its riches, whether it's a private beach, a hidden café, or a story about its maritime history.

During my first visit, I made the rookie mistake of foregoing breakfast before touring. By midday, I was starving and ate a sandwich on a seat overlooking the port. A local walking his dog stopped to chat, gave his favorite lunch spots, and even suggested a better photo location. That's the beauty of Ramsgate: a friendly face and a terrific tip are always around the corner.

So, go on and enjoy Ramsgate like the clever traveler you are. You'll depart with memories, maybe a few local words, and a strong desire to return for more.

CONCLUSION

As your Ramsgate trip comes to an end, I hope you leave with a heart full of memories and possibly a little sand in your shoes (a badge of valor, actually). Ramsgate has a way of leaving an impression, whether it's via the kindness of its people, the beauty of its coastline, or the unexpected moments you'll never forget.

Wrapping Up Your Ramsgate Adventure

Let's take a moment to reflect on all of your wonderful experiences.

The Sunrise at East Cliff: Did you see the golden rays that illuminated the Royal Harbour? If you missed it, that's simply a reason to return.

Coastal Walks: Perhaps you wandered the Viking Coastal Trail or discovered a hidden cove. I bet you felt like the star of your coastal film.

History and Heritage: From the Royal Harbour to St. Augustine's Abbey, you've passed through centuries of history. Perhaps you even traveled into the gloomy Ramsgate Tunnels, where ghosts from the past still resonate.

Food and Drink: Have you found your new favorite fish and chip restaurant? Or maybe you found the perfect Kentish ale? If you leave Ramsgate without food baby, I think you didn't strive hard enough.

This beautiful seaside jewel has a habit of surprising you around every corner. One moment you're admiring a Victorian landmark, and the next you're laughing with a local about how to pronounce "Thanet" (Thann-it, in case you were wondering).

Share Your Experience!

Traveling is about both the stories we bring home and the memories we make. So, before Ramsgate becomes simply another location on your map, take a moment to share your experience.

Social Media

Post your greatest photographs to Instagram, Facebook, or TikTok. Ramsgate's majestic cliffs, vibrant port, and golden beaches make it a photographer's paradise. Don't forget to add hashtags like #RamsgateAdventures or #CoastalTreasures—you might even inspire others to visit!

Travel Reviews

Your feedback is important! Whether you slept in a quaint bed and breakfast or dined at a local pub, submitting a review on sites like TripAdvisor or Google Maps benefits other tourists (and small businesses). If you enjoyed that obscure café or eccentric souvenir shop, let them know!

Travel Journals and Blogs

If you enjoy writing, you should try chronicling your vacation. What makes Ramsgate special to you? Was it the welcoming inhabitants, the magnificent scenery, or a humorous experience you'll never forget? Sharing your experience is an excellent way to relive your adventure while also motivating others.

Why You Will Want to Come Back

Here's the thing about Ramsgate: there's always more to see. Maybe you didn't have time to visit nearby Broadstairs or Margate, or perhaps you're already fantasizing about another feast of delicious seafood by the harbor.

I find Ramsgate's charm alluring. During one visit, I spent hours watching boats come and depart from the Royal Harbour. The next time, I went on a local walking tour and discovered stories I hadn't heard before. Ramsgate feels familiar, but there is always something new to uncover.

Additionally, Ramsgate changes with the seasons. Summer visits may include busy beaches and bustling festivals, but winter trips may include tranquil walks and pleasant evenings. If you enjoyed your current experience, consider what it would be like in another season.

Final Thoughts

As you pack your things and ready to depart Ramsgate, take a moment to enjoy your surroundings one final time. Perhaps it's the sound of seagulls calling in the distance, the salty breeze brushing against your face, or the sight of the harbor sparkling in the evening sunlight.

Leaving Ramsgate may be bittersweet, but remember that the finest part about any journey is that it leaves you wanting more. Ramsgate will be there to welcome you back whenever you are ready.

Until then, bring with you the spirit of this seaside treasure—its history, beauty, and eternal charm. Ramsgate has a way of lingering with you long after you've left, much like the sun's warmth on your skin or the laughter shared over dinner.

Safe travels, and remember that Ramsgate is more than simply a destination to visit; it is a place you will always want to return to.

Now go ahead and spread the word about this seaside beauty. And who knows? Perhaps we'll see each other here again. I'll be the one with a coffee in hand, watching the waves come in.

Printed in Dunstable, United Kingdom